Aug 200'

To
Paige

Love Uncle Shawn
&
Grandma C

I Love The Alphabet

written & illustrated by

Dar Hosta

Brown Dog Books
Flemington, New Jersey

Published by Brown Dog Books
PO Box 2196 Flemington, NJ 08822

ISBN 0-9721967-1-4

The illustrations in this book were created using collage, oil pastel, colored pencil and a digital graphics tablet. The type is Century Gothic.

Also by Dar Hosta, *I Love The Night*

Special Thanks to Jim and Rita Tadych, Editors and Parents Extraordinaire

Printed in Mexico

For My Husband, Lou,
My A to Z Guy

Come on in!

Hi there!

I love the alphabet.
I absolutely do.

I love the alphabet.
How about you?

Aa Acrobatic alligators, toesies in the air.

Bb Busy baby bumblebees
In their underwear.

Cats are in the kitchen,
making tea and cakes.

Dd
Doggy's best days
are full of sticks and lakes.

Ee Elevator won't go up with Elephant inside.

Ff Five fancy fish
on a roller coaster ride.

Hh Hippo's feeling happy underneath the apple tree.

Ii

Iguanas on an igloo
are feeling rather icy.

Jj Jaguars in jammies
share their jellybeans so nicely.

Kk

Kangaroos play peek-a-boo in a field of flowers.

...one, two, three, four, five, six...

Ll Llama in a leotard
dances in spring showers.

Mm

Two mischievous monkeys mambo on the moon.

Nn Nine hungry newts are looking for a spoon.

In and out of water, otters splashing with wet feeties.

Pp

Porcupines make valentines
for all their special sweeties.

Qq Quail's favorite quilt is cuddly and cozy.

Rr Rabbits on the riverbank play ring-around-the-rosie.

Ss Slinky, slithery snakes
are swinging from the stars.

Tt Two striped tigers
carry moonbeams home in jars.

Uu
In a fairy tale forest,
a unicorn prances around.

Vv

Vole is eating vegetables from a home under the ground.

Ww Wiggly little wombats are making birthday wishes.

Xx
Pelican gets an **X**-ray
but the fishes were delicious!

Let's get out of here!

Yodel-ay-hee-hoo! Yodel-ay-hee-hoo! Yodel-ay-hee-hoo! Yodel-ay-hee-

Yy Yak is yodeling, way up high, on mountain tippy tops.

Zz Zebra's in the candy shop for swirly lollipops.

Zollipops
10¢

Oh, yes I love the alphabet.
Oh, yes I really do!

Oh, yes, I love the alphabet!
Now, how about **YOU**?